OUT OF ONE EYE

OUT OF ONE EYE

THE ART OF

KIT WILLIAMS

Harmony Books/New York

First published in the United States by Harmony Books, a division of Crown Publishers, Inc., 225 Park Avenue South,
New York, New York 10003 and represented in Canada by the Canadian MANDA Group
Originally published in Great Britain by Jonathan Cape Ltd., 32 Bedford Square, London WC1B 3EL
Harmony and colophon are trademarks of Crown Publishers, Inc.

Manufactured in Italy

Library of Congress Cataloging-in-Publication Data

Williams, Kit.
Out of one eye.
1. Williams, Kit – Themes, motives. 2. Fantasy in
art. I. Title.
N6797.W55A4 1986   709'.2'4   86-14923
ISBN 0-517-56431-9

10 9 8 7 6 5 4 3 2 1

First American Edition

INTRODUCTION

I have never been able to shut my eyes without seeing pictures, persistent projections showing details of tantalising new things to make. Even as a small child my fantasies were about transferring pictures from my mind, through my hands and into reality. It was as if the only way I could feel alive was to surround myself with objects of my own invention.

My earliest memory is of being taken from the countryside where I lived to London to visit my maternal grandparents. Of London, I remember nothing, except being taken 'across the water' by my grandfather. He was one of seven O'Sullivan brothers who sailed the Seven Seas. He had been a ship's carpenter, but when I knew him he owned a small tobacconist's shop in Plumstead High Street. He was a large, round man and drank black beer with a creamy top. I would skim a little off this froth with my finger and eat it like candy floss. It tasted horrid. Grandfather laughed and I pretended to like it.

The water to be crossed was the Thames, oily grey and stinking in those days. Our 'ship' was the Woolwich ferry. It was one of two paddle-ferries that carried vehicles and passengers across the river. Huge paddle-wheels churned up the murky waters, making them froth and foam. Sometimes the wind carried away pieces of foam and sent them, like dirty yellow swans, scudding across the river. The size and noise of the great paddle-wheels were unforgettable. They induced a terrifying tingle of excitement. If you shrieked as loud as you could, nothing could be heard above the violent crashing. It was like screaming silence. However, in contrast to the bitterly cold wind and the noise of outside, the inside of the ship was a different world. A companionway allowed the passengers access through the engine-room. Here was a thick, hot atmosphere with the spit, splutter and smell of oil on hot brass bearings, the bubble and hiss of steam oozing from moving joints. The noise from outside could still be heard in a muffled sort of way, but the gigantic parts of this huge reciprocating engine rose and sank into the dark depths of the ship almost silently. If I had known the word 'universe', I would have realised that this was its centre and the source of all its power. To be totally surrounded by such an engine was the most awe-inspiring experience of my young life. To be architect and captain of such a vessel was to be master of the world.

5

My childhood dreams were never born in the cinema or within the pages of story-books. Swashbuckling might have been fine for others, but not for me! I would stand quietly in the shadows whilst the Queen unveiled my latest invention to wildly cheering crowds. In my mind I sailed the globe in ships with revolving sails, like windmills, which drove thrashing paddle-wheels. I would astound the world by coming first at Le Mans in my own design of rocket-powered racing car. I visited distant planets in spacecraft powered by the cathode rays emitted from television tubes. To have been a romantic child during the 1950s and early '60s, when science was the great romance and men could safely solve all the world's problems with their science and resourcefulness, was a very fine thing. The 'sputnik' had been launched and whole families paraded out at dusk to try and see the tiny flashes of light that denoted its passing. Washing-machines became 'fully automatic'. Hovercraft levitated a few inches and slithered across land and water alike.

One day, in the window of a local garage, there stood with all its doors and bonnet open – a Mini-car. As a schoolboy, my nose pressed against the glass, I marvelled at it. The engine was mounted sideways, the transmission and steering in the front wheels, and the body just folded around the people like a parcel. Brilliant!! But I hadn't invented it. I *had* invented the elastic-powered bicycle that was wound up by a spin-drier and pedalled itself to and from school. I had helped bring electrification to the lawn-mower, which now mowed at a sporting trot. I had made the first orange box television set complete with twenty controls, which were operated by plastic knitting-needles protruding from the top of the set like a multicoloured porcupine. Different and interesting things happened to the picture and sound when the needles were twiddled. My mother gradually accepted the machine and it was the first television in our house. She would astound the neighbours with her dexterity on the knitting-needles.

The hub of my activities was a shed attached to my father's garage – 'my workshop'. Although I made a regular physical appearance at school, my thoughts never accompanied me. They remained firmly in the shed.

In the world of Swiss Army pocket-knives and grass-snakes in shoe boxes there is one schoolboy achievement that ranks above all others . . . the acquisition of gunpowder. One day the word went out that Kit Williams was 'in the market for a certain formula'. Later that week behind the school pottery a transaction took place. A small piece of folded paper changed hands for a rear bicycle wheel with a three-speed hub.

Webster's Dictionary helped prove the formula but, more important, also supplied unexplosive uses for all the ingredients. Saltpetre was bought for rabbit skin curing, and flowers of sulphur for the preparation of a foot bath. Armed with these substances, plus an ample supply of artroom charcoal, I repaired to the shed.

A succession of deafening bangs, volumes of choking smoke and the eventual scorching of a considerable oak tree ended in a hastily arranged compromise.

It was decided by myself and the whole family that I should go away to sea, where I could blow things up in safety. My sixteenth year found me rather short and underweight, with extremely unconventional eyesight and still very much a boy. I was now about to go down to the sea in ships and serve my time before the mast – a junior radio electrical mechanic in Her Majesty's Royal Navy! After all my years of mental truancy from school I was barely able to read or write. Fortunately this new world in which I found myself seemed wholly concerned with pictures – beautiful linear constructions in pure logic.

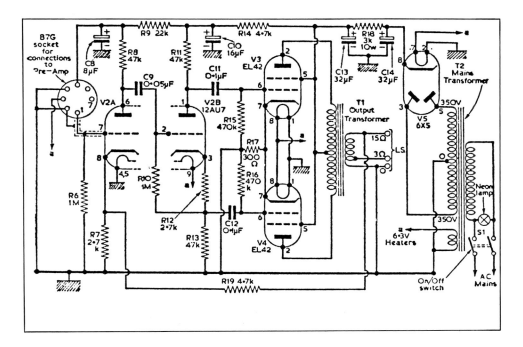

These circuit diagrams imprinted themselves upon my mind. Within their labyrinths I learnt to communicate with ships on the other side of the world and, with electronic eyes, pierced the thickest fog. Thinking like this in pictures suited me well.

In the early years of my childhood there was a boy's weekly comic called *The Eagle*. Its stories of football and adventure in space were mere tales and hardly worth the effort of reading. What did captivate me were their amazing 'dissected pictures', in which famous locomotives and delta-winged aircraft were drawn in such a way as to show all working parts and their interrelationship. I had learnt to read such drawings the way others read words, and I could mentally reassemble the machines into full working order. I thank *The Eagle* for this early visual training and have no envy for the trigger-finger reflexes developed by the children of today from their video games.

A DISSECTED PICTURE OF A
MORRIS MINI-MINOR, FROM
THE EAGLE, 5 DECEMBER 1959

Having completed naval training, I was assigned to my first ship and flew for the first time, half-way around the world to Singapore, and never once took my eyes from the aeroplane's window. Finally, after years of expectation and months of training, I found myself on a real ship in the South China Sea and, with the mysteries of the Orient so close at hand, I discovered a new experience . . . boredom! It had never occurred to me how circumscribed shipboard life would be. My job was to repair the ship's radio and radar equipment when it went wrong. For interminably long hours of watch-keeping I was forced to make up the fourth hand in card games and listen to detailed accounts of fanciful journeys under the mini-skirt. There was no escaping to the shed now, nowhere to practise the secret arts of invention. All my personal possessions had to fit, Bristol fashion, into a 'kit' bag.

For a short time my inventive urges were gratified by ingeniously modifying and experimenting with the essential equipment on Her Majesty's Warship. The investigation into the unexpected responses from previously reliable machinery eventually found me out and, with this pleasure denied by enforced deck-scrubbing and pot-scouring, it was time to think again. Having been let down by science, I compiled a list of alternative careers to pursue in this environment, limited by no funds, no equipment and nowhere to store anything. Economy was my watchword, and at the top of the list came Philosopher. The ship's library was not very forthcoming. It proffered only two volumes under Philosophy – Nietzsche and Bertrand Russell. I withdrew the entire section and retired to my bunk. Two days later I emerged. I crossed Philosopher off the list. Next in line came Artist. I could become a visual philosopher!

The task was now to satisfy my fundamental scientific inventiveness and curiosity through the sketch pad and pencil. The vision of an artist in an attic with a nude model and a bottle of absinthe was romantically attractive but practically out of the question. Nature provided ample questions for the scientist to answer, and it seemed to me at that time

8

that the bridge between the scientific process and the artistic was easily crossed. An artist simply tries to solve problems of his own invention.

I set about analysing vision and perception like a scientific exercise. Since life aboard ship was artistically barren, my shore leaves turned into expeditions in which I hungrily sought out everything that was extraordinary and unfamiliar. I visited Hindu temples, and mosques, and I studied jade carvings and Chinese dragons in street theatre. I sought out ancient monuments and giant Buddhas. Singapore is a land of different nationalities, cultures and religions, and every day a festival was celebrated by some section of the community. I saw highly coloured and ornately decorated lorries speeding through the streets accompanied by wild music and fire-crackers. I was told these were Chinese funerals, when people went to their graves with all their worldly possessions beautifully made in coloured paper to accompany them through fire into the next world. I witnessed with delight the Indian festival of *Holi* when people squirt each other with coloured water and powder paint. I walked bewildered through the thoroughly outrageous extravaganza of the Tiger Balm Gardens.

EARTHLY TEMPTATIONS —
CHARACTERS FROM THE
TIGER BALM GARDENS

SINKING FERRY — SCENE FROM THE TIGER BALM GARDENS

Everywhere I turned there was architecture resembling exotic fruit, and sampans looking like tattered brown moths blown on to the water and unable to escape.

Uncomprehending, I was excited by these ancient, compelling images. I wondered if there was a visual language which could transcend time and culture. As my interest in painting increased, so my disillusion with the romance of the sea and the rigours of naval life developed. Getting out of the Navy proved to be much more difficult than getting in and, by the time my freedom was attained, I had progressed from pencil and paper on to canvas and paint.

For the next seven years I earned a living in factories during the day and painted five hours every night. During these years I continued to develop my ideas and pursue my explorations. I became increasingly fascinated by an awareness that in everyday language one constantly conjures up images from a visual vocabulary stored in the memory. The subtlety and complexity of this image-making intrigued me and led me to wonder at what stage a visual vocabulary is attained and can be used conceptually. Small children seem to be able to use a complex visual vocabulary long before they have mastered linguistic skill. It is interesting to reflect that many artists are attracted to the strong formative images gained in early childhood.

I thought much about an 'innate visual memory' in which was stored not only the sexual imagery necessary to instigate procreation, but also many other images, such as fire, fresh running water, the movement and form of wild animals and the greenness of plants. These I thought could be as visually attractive as feminine beauty, whereas images of stagnation, putrefaction and disease were naturally repulsive. It all seemed to suggest that our fine concept of beauty is litle more than an evolutionary trick to aid the survival of the species. I believed that if I used these elementary images my work would be understood by everyone, almost subconsciously, regardless of time or culture. It seemed sad that to understand twentieth-century painting you need first to have a diploma in the history of twentieth-century art.

I became interested in dance, especially the round dance, in which people seem to be putting themselves in tune with the seasons and the cyclical nature of the universe. I queried Renaissance perspective and questioned the rules of composition, media and method. I thought about changing attitudes towards nakedness and the different approaches to painting it.

Art, it seemed, was as curious as science, and although one doesn't need to justify a reason to paint with doctrine, my early ideas were substance enough to begin the life of a raw painter.

Patterned Plate

61 × 122 CM. (24 × 48 IN.)   1967

Innocent of artistic techniques, this naïve allegory was the first painting I completed after leaving the Navy. It was worked on the smooth side of an unprimed hardboard panel. The dark absorbent surface proved most unsympathetic as a ground for oil paint, and after many painstaking months of struggling with the picture I realised that technique and method are as important as content.

Series of nine paintings

51 × 76 CM. (20 × 30 IN.) 1969

'Pinball', worked on stretched and primed canvas, is one of nine pictures based on three horizontal lines.

The pictures are very two-dimensional, like Egyptian wall paintings, and the deliberate detailing of small elements of ephemera appears almost hieroglyphic.

The problems of composition, perspective and landscape were reduced to three horizontal lines in order to explore a cool, detached attitude towards subject matter.

CINEMA (no. 6)

PINBALL (no. 5)

LUNCH WITH GULLS (no. 7)

Sunbathers

40.5 × 122 CM. (16 × 48 IN.) 1970

An interest in the way sunlight is absorbed and reflected by the human body led eventually to an analysis of the type of photograph used in travel brochures. These photographs are basically all the same. They extol the virtue of an hotel or beach by placing in front of it a bikini-clad model sipping a Martini or rising from the pool. If these elements of a picture are disregarded there remains what the photographer would consider his 'acceptable' background. Tiny dramas can be seen to be taking place over a shoulder or in the crook of a leg, and the candid nature of these images makes them visually exciting. By painting these small areas several thousand times their actual size, many interesting observational problems are presented.

Seaside

86.5 × 86.5 CM. (34 × 34 IN.) 1970

Using a microscope it is possible to separate the different coloured ink dots used in printing travel brochure pictures. The number, size and colour of the dots in any given area are the constituent components of the apparent shade or hue seen by the naked eye. Interesting experiments in colour mixing can be made using this information, and the significance of transparent and opaque colours then becomes obvious.

Looking at very small portions of print, it is difficult to determine the significance of each little mark, but in a finished painting the eye may suddenly decipher an image.

For instance, the abstract area to the right of the yellow-haired figure is probably a man lying back down on a sunbed. His left knee and right arm are raised as he checks the time on his wrist-watch.

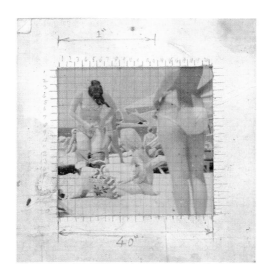

Equilibrium

101.5 × 101.5 CM. (40 × 40 IN.) 1970

It is possible to be familiar with a picture for many years and still be unaware of all its secrets. Painters love painting into their pictures little time-fuses that delight the viewer long after the initial encounter. In Pieter Bruegel's familiar painting, 'Children's Games', a small child can be seen squatting by a wall 'peeing'.

In 'Equilibrium' the tables are turned on Bruegel, the focal point of the picture innocently depicting a shy girl taking a pee 'al fresco'. The rest of the scene is quite tranquil until it is realised that a game of tennis proceeds metronome-like on the other side of the hedge.

This picture was submitted for hanging in the Royal Academy Summer Exhibition 1971 but was rejected.

DETAIL FROM BRUEGEL'S 'CHILDREN'S GAMES' 1560

Lifeboat Girl

29 × 23.5 CM. (11½ × 9¼ IN.)   1971

This small picture painted on cotton stretched over a wooden panel is an exploration into the way people look at each other.

Eye contact is a most powerful form of communication and is a compelling element in figurative painting, especially as there is a subtle difference between pictures that look at you and those that do not. A painter paints eyes looking at himself and gives them the power to confront the viewer, and in some strange way the painter looks at the viewer and the viewer looks at the painter. If the eyes are obscured or turned away, the personal link is broken and the viewer feels much more of an onlooker.

This is the first of my paintings to have a marquetry frame, and it introduced the possibility of extending the picture into the frame. Working in wood is a welcome change to the discipline of painting.

29 × 23.5 CM. (11½ × 9¼ IN.)   1974

Morris

30.5 × 46 CM. (12 × 18 IN.) 1971

A motor car, far from being merely a means of transport, is a symbol of mid-twentieth-century life. In contrast to many of the images evoked by the motor car, the Morris Minor 1000 seems the essence of homeliness.

An amusing coincidence occurred soon after the completion of this picture. A judge stated in court that 'It is impossible to be raped in the back of a Morris Minor 1000.' A framed newspaper cutting of this ruling accompanied the picture when it was subsequently sold.

The painting was exhibited at the John Moores Liverpool Exhibition in 1972, with the result that I was invited by the Portal Gallery to have my first London 'one-man show'.

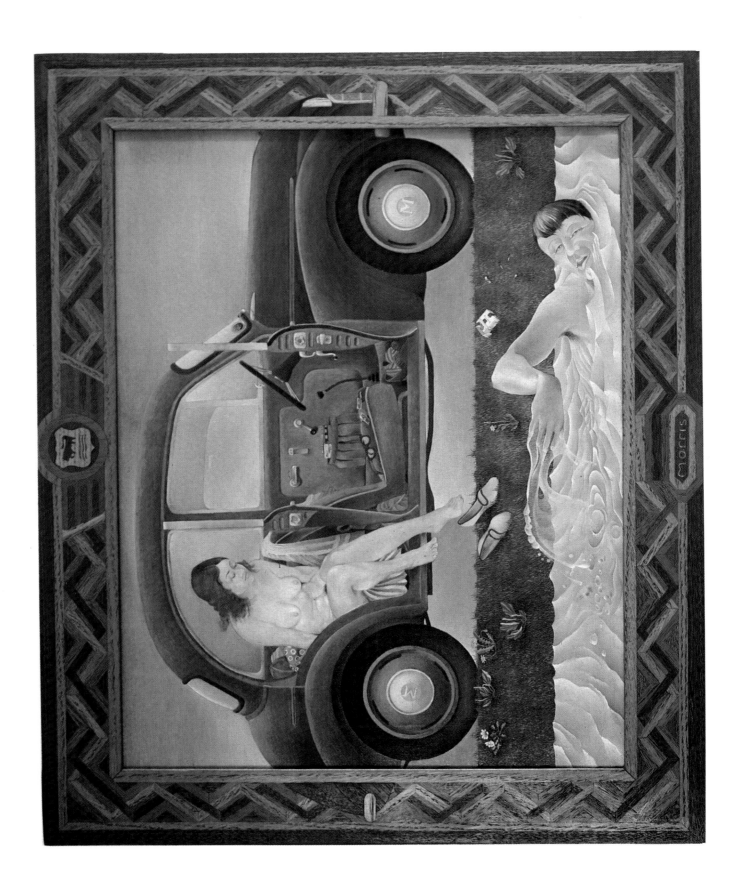

Juliet

76 × 66 CM. (30 × 26 IN.) 1972

The rigid discipline of the rectangle in which most painters work is more
likely to be due to the simplicity of its construction than to a preference
for this shape. By the use of linen-covered panels and marquetry frames,
a painting can be made any shape. The space within the picture is then
freed from being a view through a window and can be used as an
additional element of the picture.

Life in which death is often reflected is the subject of 'Juliet'. It
investigates refraction, reflection and distortion in water. A youthful
girl's face becomes a cynical death-mask when reflected by the contours
of the water's surface. This statement is echoed by a starling falling out
of the sky, its fall emphasised by the shape of the frame.

Birdcage

56 × 48 CM. (22 × 19 IN.) 1973

This painting uses its shape to create a paradox. The birdcage top and base are in the marquetry frame whilst the bars are painted *trompe-l'oeil* on the surface of the picture.

The picture is an illusion that asks the question, 'What or who is in the cage?'

'Tis just like a summer birdcage in a garden; the birds that are without despair to get in, and the birds that are within despair, and are in a consumption, for fear they shall never get out.

(The White Devil, John Webster)

Death-Defying Dora

56 × 56 CM. (22 × 22 IN.) 1973

The newspapers reported that a lady human cannonball had attempted the feat of being shot across the River Avon at Tewkesbury. She failed. It seemed a pity that her bravery should have been rewarded by such a wetting.

The painting sets out to celebrate the event, although the treatment is rather Wagnerian, a moment of ecstatic pleasure followed by violent death.

TARA TREETOPS 38 × 28 CM. (15 × 11 IN.) 1978
from *Masquerade*

Watching the Swallows Go

66 × 53.5 CM. (26 × 21 IN.) 1972

In A.E. Housman's collection of verses, *A Shropshire Lad,* one poem, 'Loveliest of trees, the cherry now', sums up the need to witness every seasonal event so that in old age the burden of regret will be lightened. In this painting an old man keeps his rendezvous with the departing swallows in autumn. To bring the landscape in which the man lives nearer to the element the birds inhabit, two rectangular shapes are married to form a 'T'. The union of land and sky, which normally only happens at the horizon, comes closer to enhance the relationship between man and birds.

Morris Interior

30.5 × 63.5 CM. (12 × 25 IN.) 1972

When a bird comes out of the vast sky into the small spaces we inhabit, it seems to change fundamentally. A bird in the bedroom causes alarm throughout the whole house.

For a fleeting moment as a bird passes through the open window of a car it takes on its aberrant nature but, on leaving, returns as a bird to the sky.

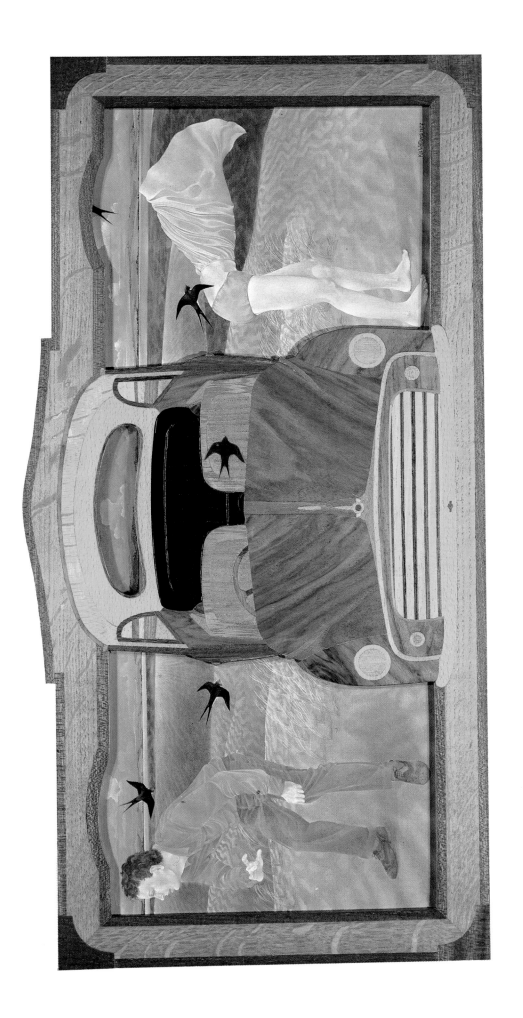

Musca Domestica

35.5 × 35.5 CM. (14 × 14 IN.) 1973

The coming of the Industrial Revolution brought with it 'leisure' and gave birth to the very British phenomenon of the knowledgeable amateur. Although to most of us the common house-fly is nothing but a nuisance, to the Amateur Naturalist it is *Musca domestica* and can command respect.

Annunciation

39.5 × 40.5 CM. (15½ × 16 IN.) 1973

Inspired by the symmetry of Victorian Gothic architecture and a couch in the Victoria and Albert Museum, this painting confronts the static tension of the artist's traditional subject, the 'Annunciation'.

The shape of the picture reflects the structural plan of a vaulted room and gives the impossible perspective and disproportion a chance to appear normal. The formality of the composition disturbs the eye and directs it towards the raven.

FRA ANGELICO'S 'ANNUNCIATION' 1408

Beach Booth

43 × 43 cm. (17 × 17 in.) 1973

There are many elements in each picture to which a painter must apply himself: composition, subject matter, mystery, colour key, scale, point of view, and so on. It has always been my opinion that in a successful painting no one of these different aspects should dominate. If it were possible to weigh all the separate ingredients in a picture and balance them equally, the picture would attain a very special ring of harmony.

In all my work this one picture comes closest to achieving this end and is therefore a particular favourite of mine.

Wether Teg*

59.5 × 56 CM. (23½ × 22 IN.) 1972

The fields of the Romney Marshes are separated by drainage ditches or dykes that collect the excess water from the land and deposit it in the river. The River Rother is slow-flowing and pleasant to swim in during the summer months. Any splashing or activity in the water always attracts the large Romney Marsh sheep which come to the bank and look on superciliously.

*A teg is a sheep in its second year.

River-Bank

84 × 84 cm. (33 × 33 in.)   1972

To prevent silting, the river on the marsh is regularly dredged. The dredgings are used to build up the banks in order to prevent the surrounding land from being flooded in winter.

When swimming in the river, one's only view is of water, bank and sky. This simple presentation of a landscape in an almost diagrammatic form allows its elements to be considered as three different textures on a flat plane.

Distress Call

26.5 × 21.5 CM. (10½ × 8½ IN.)   1973

Like a holiday snap that returns from the developers to reveal a sinister apparition unseen and unsuspected when the photograph was taken, this painting invites conjecture.

Mounted in a 'photo frame', the picture encourages the viewer to believe that at the precise moment the shot was taken a bird flew between the camera and the girl's face.

The normally attractive image of the nude figure is cancelled out by the proximity of the grotesque fledglings and the blotting-out of her face by the distressing blackbird. To supplant the missing face, the picture and the frame are mask-like in design. Shapes in the woodwork suggest ears and a mouth, while the car's wheels appear as eyes. An exact positioning of the breasts in line with the wheels causes the illusion of the eyes being transferred to the breasts. With these eyes the torso is conscious of its own vulnerability, as it looks warily out of the picture.

Bathroom

32 × 38 CM. (12½ × 15 IN.) 1973

There are many colours especially made for bathrooms. Each has its own exotic name: eau-de-Nil, rose quartz, aquamarine, avocado, and so on. Using this novel palette, the 'Bathroom' was painted for a lady who keeps her marble heart in an onyx jar.

Flora

43 × 51 CM. (17 × 20 IN.) 1973

'And yet, as she lay in the grass, all Summer's flowers grew up out of her and shone in the morning sun.'

The subject of this picture was so compelling that it later became the story in 'the book without a title' (*The Bee on the Comb*), published in 1984.

This constant re-examination of an idea is a common element within painting.

THE DEATH OF SPRING   51 × 76 CM. (20 × 30 IN.)   1980

from *The Bee on the Comb*

Morning Sequence

48 × 33 CM. (19 × 13 IN.)   1973

The early morning sunlight penetrates translucent skin to illuminate
and warm small bones and veins beneath its surface. Sweet scents rise
into the air as the dew evaporates and creatures all are eager to be
abroad.

Song of Summer

30.5 × 30.5 CM. (12 × 12 IN.) 1973

Set in an urban environment, the fiddler's song recalls the country
summers of his childhood. The words materialise as they leave his
mouth. This is an unashamedly nostalgic painting in memory of an
ever-changing Britain.

Once and Future King

66 × 56 cm. (26 × 22 in.)   1973

There is a spirit abroad that walks through the countryside playing music and changing the seasons. Every once in a while the Season-changer stops to take refreshment, but the growth of new life never ceases. Traditionally this mythological character is an embodiment of virility. The use of a very ordinary fellow, in middle age, suggests that everyone holds the key to his own destiny.

> For him in vain the envious seasons roll
> Who bears eternal summer in his soul.

> ('The Old Player', Oliver Wendell Holmes)

For Harry and St George

37 × 30.5 CM. (14½ × 12 IN.)   1973

In romantic imagery, like the Leda and the Swan myth, it is necessary to maintain the suspension of belief so that the full impact of the sensuality is not broken by logical considerations. Better not look too closely . . . lie back and think of England, Harry and St George!

Gooseman

25.5 × 18 CM. (10 × 7 IN.) 1972

A man with a figurehead of a goose rises confidently and triumphantly from the mysterious depths of the sea. The enigmatic sea swallows disaster, leaving no visible trace of her history. Sunken secrets lure men irresistibly to explore the dark fathoms. Only when she chooses does the sea offer up her plunder, scoured and broken on some distant shore. A man who woos the sea only for her dowry courts death.

In the Garden

51 × 51 CM. (20 × 20 IN.)   1974

Even in Paradise old Adam suffers a plague of cabbage-white butterflies.
As the good sun shines, Eve and the tomatoes ripen and a tiger
obligingly strolls through the vegetables to hide their naked
embarrassment.

Volti Subito

30.5 × 25.5 × 7.5 CM. (12 × 10 × 3 IN.) 1974

Place this two-sided picture a few inches in front of a mirror on a mantelshelf and its trigger is set.

It lies in wait until suddenly, its duplicity unveiled, it shocks the shockable or delights the delightful.

Box

18 × 25.5 × 14 CM. (7 × 10 × 5½ IN.)   1971

One dilemma confronting an unknown artist is — how to get his work seen. The 'Box' was conceived in an attempt to solve this problem. It was realised that if an exhibition demonstrating all the artist's skills could be made so small that it was easily portable, the embarrassment of walking into a gallery with paintings under one's arm would simply not exist. Far better to have a small box inside a paper bag! Who is to know that it is not lunch or a little shopping? This way it is possible to pop into many galleries, getting the feel of them and even conversing with the lizard behind the desk.

Painting, carving, marquetry, cabinet-making, casting, etching, lock-making and tailoring all inside one box! This 'apprentice piece' was the first work completed by me as a full-time artist and took nine months to finish. It formed a foundation stone that marked a definite beginning.

Its use as a means of introduction was superseded when the Portal Gallery owners invited me to exhibit as a result of having seen 'Morris' in Liverpool.

The box was at first considered too *risqué* for exhibition and did not appear until the third London show. Tom Maschler, Chairman of Jonathan Cape, saw the exhibition. He then broached the possibility of a book.

It could be said that the box gave birth to *Masquerade*.

Eucharist

71 × 66 CM. (28 × 26 IN.) 1974

The wishes of the Catholic Church and the day-dreams of grubby-kneed boys have little in common. To be dressed up in pleats and ruffles and made to serve at Sunday Mass does nothing to mollify such a child. A serving-boy is about the same height as people kneeling at an altar rail and, viewed from the vending-end, communion is a bizarre procession of tongues. Blind and obscene creatures that all week have clacked and wagged, licked and tasted, find themselves naked and exposed. They hang out, they loll, they gag in the throat, they flutter, they swell and point and prod, and none is content until crowned by a small white petal and can return again to a slippery darkness.

This painting remembers the day that a young Irish nun knelt at the altar rail.

Patience and the Passing of Time

58.5 × 43 CM. (23 × 17 IN.) 1974

A circle and square join together to unite a two-dimensional plane with a three-dimensional space.

In the same way the Ace of Clubs, wearing nothing but jet beads, awakens in Patience the memory of another age and another place, in the days when all her beads hung on one string.

Advancing Ripe Harvest

61 × 47 CM. (24 × 18½ IN.) 1974

Lean and anxious, the spirit of germination toils in the harsh air of early spring. As the year advances and the hours of day become longer, there is time to sit awhile in fruitful contemplation, until a fleeing hare heralds the harvest and the swish of scythes and men.

IRIS   51 × 38 CM. (20 × 15 IN.)   1973

Swing

29 × 17 × 12.5 CM. (11½ × 6¾ × 5 IN.) 1974

This small piece of table sculpture invites a push. Pivoted at the top, it reciprocates. A silhouette of the figure is worked in marquetry on the reverse side of the sculpture, so that even from the back one is made aware of the direction of the sunlight.

Globe

19 CM. HIGH × 10 CM. DIAMETER (7½ × 4 IN.)   1975

How could it be possible to paint whilst travelling rough in India? Oil paint takes days to dry hard enough to be touched, during which time it must be kept dust-free. The solution . . . ? A wooden sphere suspended inside a second outer sphere.

The hard outer case enabled the inner ball to be painted on at any time. When simply snapped shut it could be thrown in a knapsack in the knowledge that nothing could spoil the painting.

On returning to England, the outer ball was embellished with marquetry and a fancy brass stand. Inside the lid is painted a dragon. His head is made of brass and the teeth locate with a cog on the spindle of the painted ball. When a brass catch is released and the globe opened, the dragon's teeth set the inner ball spinning.

In a dance of life, each painted animal leaps out of the mouth of another.

Orb

30.5 CM. HIGH × 15 CM. DIAMETER (12 × 6 IN.)   1974

Following the success of the 'Globe', 'Orb' was conceived as a much more sophisticated interpretation of the same idea.

Gilded and stone-studded animals on the outside of an outer sphere are attached by threaded studs. Inside, the studs are secured by screw-threaded silver stars. The stars and animals relate to one another in the same way as the celestial constellations in the night sky. The fastening is a man with his head in a lion's mouth. Depress the lion's tail and his jaws open to release the man's head and open the orb. Among the stars inside the lid there is a full moon with its craters and seas correctly placed. The painted ball is heavily weighted equatorially with lead and, when spun by the thumb-wheel in the stand, spins for many minutes on a single ball-bearing.

Like the great Hindu deities, each character in the dance rides on his or her own animal 'car'.

Orrery

84 × 66 × 23 CM. (33 × 26 × 9 IN.)   1975

An orrery is a complicated clockwork mechanism showing the movements of the planets and their moons around the sun. Invented around 1700 by George Graham, it was made by the instrument-maker Rowley for Prince Eugène. Rowley also made a copy for Charles Boyle, the fourth Earl of Orrery, in whose honour it was named.

In the centre of this orrery is a brass lion with a sunray mane. By turning the handle on his feet clockwise he can be turned in that direction, while the painting and lettered surround turn anticlockwise in a ratio of three revolutions of the lion to one of the painting.

A brass thrush cursor at the top of the orrery points to the letters as they pass. Starting at 'dance', the riddle reads . . . 'Dance three rings the song thrush sings, add one a day to ensnare the hare.'

In obedience to this inscription the lion is turned three times a day, causing the big wheel to turn once. If the outer ring is then moved on one letter, the moon in the little window will change phase in step with the real moon in the sky. The hare in many mythologies is the moon's messenger.

There are fifty-nine letters in the riddle so that when the turning procedure has continued for twenty-nine days the picture has actually turned twenty-nine and a half times, thus making up the extra half-day in the lunar month.

After twelve lunar months a brown hare will jump over the moon and in the second year a white one will do the same.

Orrery to a Minor Planet

46 × 35.5 × 12.5 CM. (18 × 14 × 5 IN.) 1977

This orrery functions fully automatically. Air entering the pierced grille at the bottom either warms or cools a metal ball directly behind it. The free flow of air is encouraged by the grid at the top of the box.

The temperature of the metal ball is conducted via a copper strip to a bimetallic spiral, once part of an automatic choke on a Volkswagen car. Any change in temperature causes the bimetallic spiral to contract or expand, and as it does so a spindle at its centre rotates. These small movements are magnified by a gear train to turn the planet, a balsa wood ball. In this way the planet is always revolving, as the amount of temperature change required to do the work is very small.

Painted on the surface of the planet are its inhabitants, a succession of animal musicians each with a different instrument.

Triptych

(CLOSED) 40.5 × 40.5 × 7.5 CM. (16 × 16 × 3 IN.) 1976

Fascinated by things going round and round in a never-ending dance, the triptych was my attempt to achieve the same result without using mechanical motion. The flautist seen leaving the picture on the left enters again on the right. When the triptych is closed his two halves are joined, completing the circle that forms the dance.

This piece is designed to remain closed, revealing its intricate marquetry front panel. By manipulating the wooden block puzzle in the middle, the triptych may be opened for special occasions.

Firmament

79 × 71 CM. (31 × 28 IN.) 1979

Egyptian wall-painting, concerned as it was with meticulously tabulating all aspects of daily and spiritual life, sometimes provided answers to profound questions with images of universal simplicity.

In an Egyptian creation myth Nut, the creator of the universe, was supported by Shu, the Air god, who also separated her from her consort Geb, the Earth god.

This painting was inspired by the Nut image but was changed subtly by the depiction of a palace gardener, seen in a Persian miniature, who bends to plant a rose. With earth and air, plants and animals, and the fishes of the ocean, the starry vault of the firmament encompasses all.

SHU SUPPORTING NUT

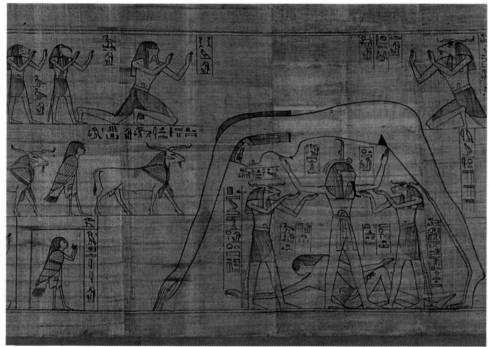

DETAIL FROM 'FIRMAMENT'

DETAIL FROM 'FIRMAMENT'

Impudent Encounter

56 × 53.5 CM. (22 × 21 IN.) 1977

The use of high-speed photography allows the fleeting instant to be observed in minute detail.

By simulating this technique it is possible to paint the half-imagined incident, the time when it is impossible to believe one's own eyes. So much of perception is not what the eyes have actually seen but images from the imagination triggered by visual fragments received by the brain. We appear to live as much in an imagined environment as a real one, looking 'out of one eye' whilst looking inward with the other.

Mistletoe Oak

38 × 40.5 CM. (15 × 16 IN.) 1976

The Druids held the oak tree in great veneration as a symbol of life, and mistletoe growing on an oak was especially revered.

Framed in the same elaborate shape as 'Firmament', this picture portrays the ever-changing state of matter. With each organism feeding upon others, atoms and molecules are constantly being recycled from one life form into another.

THE MAN WHO PLAYS MUSIC THAT MAKES THE WORLD GO ROUND
from *Masquerade*

38 × 28 CM. (15 × 11 IN.) 1978

Reflection

66 × 56 CM. (26 × 22 IN.) 1976

Only a percentage of light hitting the surface of a pool will be reflected. The remainder is absorbed and dispersed by the water and particles suspended in it. This gives reflections in water their mystery, so different from the sharp image in the bathroom mirror.

This painting is a logical deduction of what might appear in certain light conditions. The reflection was not derived photographically.

HONEY TINTED POOL   61 × 38 CM. (24 × 15 IN.)   1981
from *The Bee on the Comb*

No Ball

66 × 46 cm. (26 × 18 in.)   1974

This technical term is used by the umpire in the game of cricket –
meaning an incorrect delivery of the ball by the bowler.

> Sport that wrinkled Care derides,
> And Laughter holding both his sides.
> Come, and trip it as ye go
> On the light fantastic toe.

(*L'Allegro*, John Milton)

VILLAGE CRICKET   20 × 56 cm. (8 × 22 in.)   1974

The Princess and the Pea

46 × 38 cm. (18 × 15 in.) 1976

The fairy-tale in which, to prove the legitimacy of a girl purporting to be a princess, a pea is placed under twenty mattresses on her bed, has always been a delightful and amusing notion. A real princess would be disturbed by the pea and wouldn't sleep, whereas an ordinary girl would be unable to feel it.

This painting reconstructs the scene, the turned sides of the frame supporting the canopy of her four-poster bed. The writhing tendrils of the pea-motif backdrop represent her royal discomfort.

Three animal-shaped pictures

HEDGEHOG 15 × 28 CM. (6 × 11 IN.) 1976
BROWN HAIRSTREAK 56 × 28 CM. (22 × 11 IN.) 1977
BADGER 18 × 38 CM. (7 × 15 IN.) 1979

The height of a man's eyes as he walks along is very different from that of animals living in the same landscape.

These three pictures are an attempt to depict the world as seen from the perspective of the creatures they portray.

Erotic Orb

15 CM. HIGH × 10 CM. DIAMETER (6 × 4 IN.)   1975

This wind-up fantasy uses clockwork to animate a bedroom episode. All the works and painted scene are contained within a turned elm ball. A lens allows light to enter, illuminating the diorama, whilst another gives a clear view of the happenings.

The winding mechanism includes a variable timing device, so that it is possible to extend the length of the performance from a few seconds to an hour!

The key is kept in a drawer in the wooden base on which the ball sits when not in use.

Adam and Eve Box

(CLOSED) 35.5 × 35.5 × 35.5 CM. (14 × 14 × 14 IN.) 1974

A mahogany box with a yew lid contains paintings of Adam and Eve plus a bronze ball. The ball is set in gimbals to enable it to be moved in any direction.

The surface of the ball is inlaid with silver and gold animals with a continuous ribbon of the names from the genealogy in Genesis enchased between them. 'Mizraim begat Ludim, and Lehabim, and Naphtuhim, who begat . . . ' and so on. After the bronze was treated with heat and oxides, darkening it to contrast with the brilliant gold and silver, semi-precious stones set in gold were applied as the final embellishment before fixing into the gimbals.

One day, long after the box was completed, it was standing on a table in a shady room. A thin shaft of sunlight came through a gap in the curtains and fell upon the bronze ball. Gold and silver animals were projected all over the walls and ceiling as if the room were a planetarium for an unknown galaxy.

Noah's Ark

35.5 CM. HIGH (14 IN.) 1976

Every year the Portal Gallery has a special Christmas show based upon a theme. One year Noah's Ark was chosen. I set to and made a little ship, ribbing it and planking it in the same way Noah must have done. I gave it a deck and a wheel-house and mounted it on a carved wooden dolphin.

The Noah's Ark story is traditionally depicted with the animals entering decorously two by two, as in the nursery song. Such renderings choose to overlook the prime reason for the animals' invitation. I chose to venture 'below deck'.

Salamander

68.5 × 76 CM. (27 × 30 IN.) 1979

An elderly gentleman, living in an old people's home by the sea, is taken to the fire by his young nurse and left to doze. The spirit of fire, the Salamander, whips into life, and then consumes his dreams. When the nurse returns the old man is no longer asleep.

Truth Dare Promise

73.5 × 25.5 CM. (29 × 10 IN.)   1979

A children's game named 'truth, dare, kiss or promise' somehow captures that balance between fear and excitement which is so much a part of childhood. Each player in turn is asked a question. He or she must answer truthfully, or accept a dare, be kissed or make a promise.

What is truth? said jesting Pilate; and would not stay for an answer.

(*Essays*, Francis Bacon)

The Linnet and the Frog Bracelet

5 CM. DIAMETER (2 IN.)   1984

By the side of a shady pool stood a tall, ancient tree and on the topmost twig of this tree perched a bird that sang and sang the whole day long. The bird was a rather gaudy linnet who wore a bright red flash on the top of his head as if it were a ruby crown. His songs were mostly self-congratulatory, making exaggerated reference to his skills as a musician, his superior appearance and his popularity among the lady linnets. As the day progressed into evening and shadows lengthened across the pool, there came a faint but persistent sound.

Boop-boop. Boop-boop.

The linnet, who was right in the middle of his latest and most conceited composition, faltered and sang a wrong note. He stopped his singing to ascertain the source of the interruption.

Boop-boop. Boop-boop.

There it was again!

'Who is it who dares to make such a noise whilst I'm performing?' shrieked the linnet.

''Tis I,' said a little frog, sitting at the edge of the pool. 'I only sing to please.'

'Sing to please!' scoffed the linnet. 'Why, I've heard tunes played on a rusty hinge that are better than your amphibious tones!' and he laughed loudly at his own joke. 'Downright depressing, that's what you are, low creature! Who could possibly wish to hear you sing?'

'There are a few,' said the frog.

'Tell you what,' condescended the linnet, 'why don't you and I have a little competition, a sort of tuneful tournament, in which I . . . whoever is the winner stays, and you, I mean the other, must find somewhere else to sing.' He even put forward his ruby crown as a side bet, so sure was he of winning.

The tournament was arranged for the next day. The judge would be the first stranger to pass that way. The two contestants would sing and whoever most impressed the passer-by would be the winner. The linnet was up bright and early, spraying his throat with an operatic atomiser and practising complicated scales before a mirror. The frog looked on, blinkingly. At about half-past eleven a little old man in big baggy blue trousers and wooden shoes came by. He sat down to rest on a tree stump beside the pool.

'This is my chance!' thought the linnet and launched forth into his prelude. The old man seemed unaware of the music as he delved in his pockets for a tobacco pipe. By the beginning of the first movement the linnet was in fine voice and sang and sang for all his worth. The man

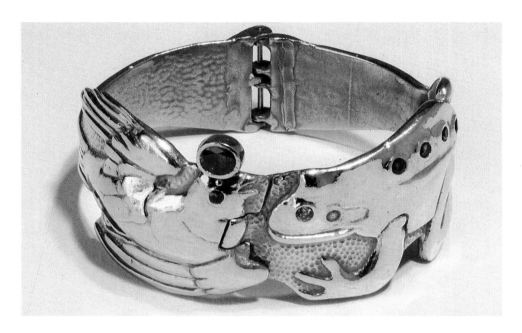

scraped the inside of the pipe with his thumbnail, blew noisily down its spout and tapped it against his heel. During the second movement the linnet entered into an emotional passage and great watery tears rolled down his cheeks, wetting the feathers on his chest. But the man only rubbed tobacco in the palm of his hand and sniffed its aroma. With great gusto and full vibrato, the linnet began the last movement while the man tamped down the tobacco in the bowl with his second finger. Throughout the coda he rummaged for matches, shook them in the box by his ear, selected one and struck it on the sole of his shoe. The linnet was exhausted, spent, all sung-out. He just clung to his branch and gasped for breath.

    The match flared and the old man touched it to the pipe. Puff-puff. Puff-puff. From quite close by came the answer. Boop-boop. Boop-boop. The old man began to smile.

    Puff-puff. Puff-puff.
    Boop-boop. Boop-boop.
    Chuckle. Puff-puff.
    Boop-boop.
    He clapped his hands and laughed aloud.
    Puff-puff.
    Boop-boop.
    The conclusion of this story is not very hard to understand to those who know that the frog is a Dutchman's nightingale.
    Puff-puff. Boop-boop.

This story was written and the solid gold bracelet made for a Dutchman to give to his wife on their wedding anniversary.

    The ruby in the linnet's crown slides up to release the catch and open the bracelet.

ACKNOWLEDGMENTS

I should like to acknowledge the help of Jessica Wilder of the Portal Gallery in finding all the pictures, and thank the individual owners of the pictures for allowing their inclusion in this book. I am also grateful to the following for permission to reproduce illustrations: the Trustees of the British Museum ('Shu Supporting Nut' from the Greenfield Papyrus); Kunsthistorisches Museum, Vienna (Bruegel's 'Children's Games'); George Newnes Ltd (circuit diagram from *Hi-Fi and Audio*); Scala/Florence (Fra Angelico's 'Annunciation'); Syndication International Ltd (dissected picture from *The Eagle*).